Also by Robert Bly

Poetry
Silence in the Snowy Fields
The Light Around the Body
The Teeth Mother Naked at Last
Jumping Out of Bed
Sleepers Joining Hands
Old Man Rubbing His Eyes
The Morning Glory
This Body Is Made of Camphor and Gopherwood
This Tree Will Be Here for a Thousand Years

Translations (Poetry)
Twenty Poems of Georg Trakl
(WITH JAMES WRIGHT)
Neruda and Vallejo: Selected Poems
(WITH JAMES WRIGHT AND JOHN KNOEPFLE)
Lorca and Jimenez: Selected Poems
Friends, You Drank Some Darkness. Martinson,
Ekelöf and Tranströmer: Selected Poems
Bashō: Twelve Poems
The Kabir Book: 44 of the Ecstatic Poems of Kabir
Twenty Poems of Rolf Jacobsen
Mirabai: Six Versions
Selected Poems of Rainer Maria Rilke

Translations (Fiction)
Hunger, by Knut Hamsun
The Story of Gösta Berling, by Selma Lagerlöf

Interviews
Talking All Morning: Collected Interviews and
        Conversations

Anthologies
Forty Poems Touching on Recent American History
The Sea and the Honeycomb: Eighty Tiny Poems
News of the Universe: Poems of Twofold
        Consciousness

The Man in the Black Coat Turns

The
Man
in the
Black Coat
Turns

poems by

Robert Bly

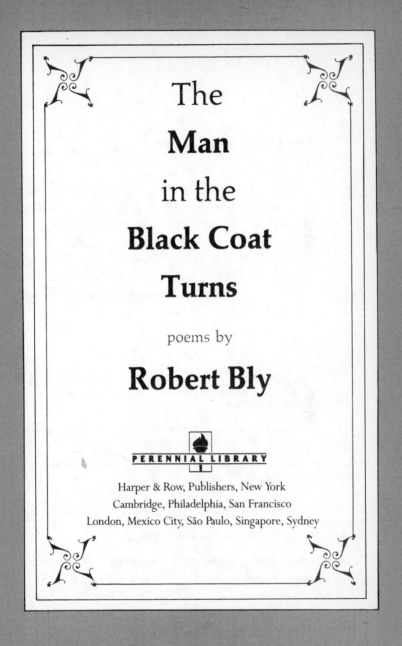

PERENNIAL LIBRARY

Harper & Row, Publishers, New York
Cambridge, Philadelphia, San Francisco
London, Mexico City, São Paulo, Singapore, Sydney

I am grateful to the editors of the following reviews, in whose pages some of these poems first appeared: *Parabola, The New Republic, Kayak, The Ohio Review, Harper's Magazine, American Poetry Review, The Iowa Review, Grove, The Cornell Review, Harvard Magazine, The Missouri Review, The Atlantic Monthly, Poetry East,* and *Brothersongs,* an anthology from Holy Cow! Press.

A hardcover edition of this book was published in 1981 by Doubleday & Company. It is hereby reprinted by arrangement with Doubleday & Company.

First PERENNIAL LIBRARY edition published 1988.

LIBRARY OF CONGRESS CATALOG CARD NUMBER: 88-45108

ISBN: 0-06-097186-X (pbk.)

88 89 90 91 92   FG   10 9 8 7 6 5 4 3 2 1

For Noah Matthew

Contents

The Man in the Black Coat Turns

I

Snowbanks North of the House

Those great sweeps of snow that stop suddenly six
    feet from the house . . .
Thoughts that go so far.
The boy gets out of high school and reads no more
    books;
the son stops calling home.
The mother puts down her rolling pin and makes no
    more bread.
And the wife looks at her husband one night at a
    party, and loves him no more.
The energy leaves the wine, and the minister falls
    leaving the church.
It will not come closer—
the one inside moves back, and the hands touch
    nothing, and are safe.

The father grieves for his son, and will not leave the
    room where the coffin stands.
He turns away from his wife, and she sleeps alone.

And the sea lifts and falls all night, the moon goes on
    through the unattached heavens alone.

The toe of the shoe pivots
in the dust . . .
And the man in the black coat turns, and goes back
    down the hill.
No one knows why he came, or why he turned away,
    and did not climb the hill.

For My Son Noah, Ten Years Old

Night and day arrive, and day after day goes by,
and what is old remains old, and what is young
remains young, and grows old.
The lumber pile does not grow younger, nor the
two-by-fours lose their darkness,
but the old tree goes on, the barn stands without help
so many years;
the advocate of darkness and night is not lost.

The horse steps up, swings on one leg, turns its body,
the chicken flapping claws onto the roost, its wings
whelping and walloping,
but what is primitive is not to be shot out into the
night and the dark.
And slowly the kind man comes closer, loses his rage,
sits down at table.

So I am proud only of those days that pass in
        undivided tenderness,
when you sit drawing, or making books, stapled,
        with messages to the world,
or coloring a man with fire coming out of his hair.
Or we sit at a table, with small tea carefully poured.
So we pass our time together, calm and delighted.

The Prodigal Son

The Prodigal Son is kneeling in the husks.
He remembers the man about to die
who cried, "Don't let me die, Doctor!"
The swine go on feeding in the sunlight.

When he folds his hands, his knees on corncobs,
he sees the smoke of ships
floating off the isles of Tyre and Sidon,
and father beyond father beyond father.

An old man once, being dragged across the floor
by his shouting son, cried:
"Don't drag me any farther than that crack on the
      floor—
I only dragged my father that far!"

My father is seventy-five years old.
How difficult it is,
bending the head, looking into the water.
Under the water there's a door the pigs
      have gone through.

Visiting the Farallones

The Farallones seals clubbed,
whales gone, tortoises
taken from islands
to fill the holds, the Empire

dying in its provincial cities,
no one to repair the baths,
farms turned over
to soldiers, the judges corrupt.

The wagon behind bouncing,
breaking on boulders, back
and forth, slowly
smashed to pieces. This crumb-

ling darkness is a reality
too, the feather
on the snow, the rooster's
half-eaten body nearby.

And other worlds I do not see:
The Old People's Home
at dusk, the slow
murmur of conversation.

The Convict and His Radio

The child left alone on the butte calls out to his
      grandmother in the pine.
She answers, the hide slips off the rack, the hatchet
      leaps up from the ground.
The buffalo gallop, the cliff lies just ahead.
Men shaped like stones lie waiting . . .
             They leap up flapping hides;
the buffalo flow over the cliff, rib
          and leg bones splinter,
a few roll down the pile and stagger off.
The prison opens at last, the convict comes out
      carrying a cardboard box.
No one can speak to him, his tongue by now is
      forgotten.
He sits alone by a black radio.
At night he cries, reaching for the small table by his
      bed.
           He does not stop all night,
he cries until dawn.

Mourning Pablo Neruda

Water is practical,
especially in
August.
Faucet water
that drops
into the buckets
I carry
to the young
willow trees
whose leaves have been eaten
off by grasshoppers.
Or this jar of water
that lies next to me
on the carseat
as I drive to my shack.
When I look down,
the seat all
around the jar
is dark,
for water doesn't intend
to give, it gives
anyway,

and the jar of water
lies
there quivering
as I drive
through a countryside
of granite quarries,
stones
soon to be shaped
into blocks for the dead,
the only
thing they have
left that is theirs.

For the dead remain inside
us, as water
remains
inside granite—
hardly at all—
for their job is to
go
away,
and not come back,
even when we ask them,
but water
comes to us—
it doesn't care
about us, it goes
around us, on the way
to the Minnesota River,

to the Mississippi River,
to the Gulf,
always closer
to where
it has to be.
No one lays flowers
on the grave
of water,
for it is not
here,
it is
gone.

II

Eleven O'Clock at Night

I lie alone in my bed; cooking and stories are over at last, and some peace comes. And what did I do today? I wrote down some thoughts on sacrifice that other people had, but couldn't relate them to my own life. I brought my daughter to the bus—on the way to Minneapolis for a haircut—and I waited twenty minutes with her in the somnolent hotel lobby. I wanted the mail to bring some praise for my ego to eat, and was disappointed. I added up my bank balance, and found only $65, when I need over a thousand to pay the bills for this month alone. So this is how my life is passing before the grave?

The walnut of my brain glows. I feel it irradiate the skull. I am aware of the consciousness I have, and I mourn the consciousness I do not have.

Stubborn things lie and stand around me—the walls, a bookcase with its few books, the footboard of the bed, my shoes that lay against the blanket tentatively, as if they were animals sitting at table, my stomach with its curved demand. I see the bedside lamp, and the thumb of my right hand, the pen my fingers hold so trustingly. There is no way to escape from these. Many times in poems I have escaped—from myself. I sit for hours and at last see a pinhole in the top of the pumpkin, and I slip out that pinhole, gone! The genie expands and is gone; no one can get him back in the bottle again; he is hovering over a car cemetery somewhere.

Now more and more I long for what I cannot escape from. The sun shines on the side of the house across the street. Eternity is near, but it is not *here*. My shoes, my thumbs, my stomach, remain inside the room, and for that there is no solution. Consciousness comes so slowly, half our life passes, we eat and talk asleep—and for that there is no solution. Since Pythagoras died the world has gone down a certain path, and I cannot change that. Someone not in my family invented the microscope, and Western eyes grew the intense will to pierce down through its darkening tunnel. Air itself is willing without pay to lift the 707's wing, and for that there is no solution. Pistons and rings have appeared in the world; valves usher gas vapor in and out of the theater box ten times a second; and for that there is no solution. Something besides my will loves the woman I love. I love my children, though I did not know them before they came. I change every day. For the winter dark of late December there is no solution.

When a man steps out at dawn, it seems to him that he has lived his whole life to create something dark. What he has created is the wine in the hold of the ship. The casks roll about when the ship rolls, and no one knows what is in them but the captain. The captain stands looking out over the taffrail in the dark, drawn by what follows in shoals behind him. Behind him, shoals of fins sail with intense forward strokes. The ship is going to a harbor the captain has chosen, and the casks are rolling. That is all we know.

The ship remained so long tied to the dock, rubbing, as the captain lay ill on his pallet in the seaman's home, imagining the covers were a Medusa with his mother's face. And one day as he woke he was already on board. It must be that he hired the seamen, and bought the supplies, while still asleep. Now the ship is moving, and what does he know about those men he has hired? What are the islands like, where they were born; whom do they kneel to at night, fanning a fire of pencil shavings? Or was it a farmhouse in Montana? Did the seaman then pass into prison, and through it, as the earthworm passes through thoughtless soil?

The ship is moving, and the wine sways in the hold. But how long has gone by already! How many men, before the captain was born, labored to produce it! First the grapes had to be brought from Europe, and a climate found, calm and protective; then ground scouted out where the grapes could be at home, difficult to discover with the unknown acids and mineral traces . . . And it takes so long for the vines to mature. And when at last the vines are grown, tough, twisted, resembling intense dwarf houses, then the owner has to wake at three in the morning to protect them from frost, and light smudge fires. The stalk of the vine slowly widens.

But the assurances others give us: "You're a good father"; "You're a good captain" . . . what do they amount to? They do nothing, however gladly we hear them, because we are not the captain. The captain is still alone on the ship, alone among the ocean-flying terns, the great hooded mergansers flopping at early dusk light over the sparse waves they have never been introduced to . . . Mist suddenly appears at mid-ocean . . . No assurances in the ocean. When a man steps out at dawn, and breathes in the air, it seems to him he has lived his whole life to create something dark!

The Dried Sturgeon

I climb down from the bridge at Rock Island, Illinois, and cross some tracks. It is October. Westward the black railway bridge makes short hops across the river. The riverbank is confused with drifted leaves, chill, the sand cold in late October.

I see a dried-out fish . . . It is a sturgeon . . . It is stiff, all its sudden motion gone. I pick it up . . . its speckled nose-bone leads back to the eyesocket . . . and behind that there is a dark hole where the gills once were.

So the darkness enters just behind the head. It is the darkness under the bunched leaves, the soothing darkness ten feet down in sand. The pine tree standing by the roadhouse holds the whole human night in one needle. The gill-hole holds the sweet dark of the hunchback's dreams, where he is straight and whole again, and the earth is flat and crooked. A virgin brings out four black stones for him from beneath her cloak.

Behind the gill opening the scales go on toward the tail. The scales are dry, swift, organized, tubular, straight and humorless as railway schedules,

the big clamp of the boxcar, tapering into sleek
womanly death.

A Bouquet of Ten Roses

The roses lift from the green strawberrylike leaves, their edges slightly notched, for the rose is also the plum, the apple, the strawberry, and the cherry. Petals are reddish orange, the color of a robin's breast if it were silk. I look down into the face of one rose: deep down inside there are somber shades, what Tom Thumb experienced so low under chairs, in the carpet-darkness . . . those growing swirls of gathering shadows, which eyes up near lamps do not see. It is the calm fierceness in the aborigine's eye as he holds his spear polished by his own palm. These inviting lamblike falmers are also the moist curtains of the part of the woman she cannot see; and the cloud that opens, swarming and parting for Adonis . . . It is an opening seen by no one, only experienced later as rain. And the rose is also the skin petals around the man's stalk, the soft umber folds that enclose so much longing; and the tip shows violet, blind, longing for company, knowing already of an intimacy the thunderstorm keeps as its secret, understood by the folds of purple curtains, whose edges drag the floor.

And in the center of the nine roses, whose doors are opening, there is one darker rose on a taller stem. It is the rose of the tumbling waters, of the strumming at night, the color of the Ethiopian tumblers who put their heads below their feet on the Egyptian waterfront, wheeling all over the shore . . . This rose is the man sacrificed yesterday, the silent one wounded under the oak, the man whose dark foot needs to be healed. He experiences the clumsy feeling that can only weep. It is the girl who has gone down to the world below, disobeying her mother, in order to bring calm to the house, traveling alone . . . and the rose windows of Chartres, the umber moss on the stag's antlers. . . .

Visiting Emily Dickinson's Grave with Robert Francis

A black iron fence closes the graves in, its ovals delicate as wine stems. They resemble those chapel windows on the main Aran island, made narrow in the fourth century so that not too much rain would drive in . . . It is April, clear and dry. Curls of grass rise around the nearby gravestones.

The Dickinson house is not far off. She arrived here one day, at fifty-six, Robert says, carried over the lots between by six Irish laboring men, when her brother refused to trust her body to a carriage. The coffin was darkened with violets and pine boughs, as she covered the immense distance between the solid Dickinson house and this plot . . .

The distance is immense, the distances through which Satan and his helpers rose and fell, oh vast areas, the distances between stars, between the first time love is felt in the sleeves of the dress, and the death of the person who was in that room . . . the distance between the feet and head as you lie down, the distance between the mother and father, through which we pass reluctantly.

My family addresses "an Eclipse every morning, which they call their 'Father.' " Each of us crosses that distance at night, arriving out of sleep on hands and knees, astonished we see a hump in the ground where we thought a chapel would be . . . it is a grassy knoll. And we clamber out of sleep, holding on to it with our hands . . .

Finding an Old Ant Mansion

The rubbing of the sleeping bag on my ear made me dream a rattlesnake was biting me. I was alone, waking the first morning in the North. I got up, the sky clouded, the floor cold. I dressed and walked out toward the pasture. And how good the unevenness of the pasture feels under tennis shoes! The earth gives little rolls and humps ahead of us . . .

The earth never lies flat, but is always thinking, it finds a new feeling and curls over it, rising to bury a toad or a great man, it accounts for a fallen meteor, or stones rising from two hundred feet down, giving a little jump for Satan, and a roll near it for Calvin . . . I turn and cut through a strip of cleared woods; only the hardwoods are still standing. As I come out into the pasture again, I notice something lying on the ground.

It's about two feet long. It is a wood-chunk, but it has open places in it, caves chewed out by something. The bark has fallen off, that was the roof . . . I lift it up and carry it home kitty-corner over the field.

When I set it on my desk, it stands. The base

is an inch or two of solid wood, only a bit eaten by the acids that lie in pastures. The top four or five inches is also solid, a sort of forehead.

In between the forehead and base there are sixteen floors eaten out by ants. The floors flung out from the central core are light brown, the color of workmen's benches, and old eating tables in Norwegian farmhouses. The open places in between are cave-dark, the heavy brown of barn stalls in November dusk, the dark the cow puts her head into at the bottom of mangers . . . A little light comes in from the sides, as when a woman at forty suddenly sees what her mother's silences as she washed clothes meant, and which are the windows in the side of her life she has not yet opened . . .

And these open places are where the ant legions labored, the antlered layers awakening, antennae brush the sandy roof ceilings, low and lanterned with the bullheat of their love, and the lively almsgivers go forth, the polished threshold passed by thousands of pintaillike feet, with their electricity for all the day packed into their solid-state joints and carapaces. Caravans go out, climbing, gelid with the confidence of landowners; and soon they are at work, right here, making delicate balconies where their eggs can pass their childhood in embroidered chambers; and the infant ants awaken to old father-worked halls, uncle-loved boards, walls that hold the sighs of the pasture, the moos of confused cows, sound of

oak leaves in November, flocks of grasshoppers pass-
ing overhead, some car motors from the road, held in
the sane wood, given shape by Osiris' love.

Now it seems to be a completed soul home.
These balconies are good places for souls to sit, in the
half-dark. If I put it on our altar, souls of the dead in
my family can come and sit now, I will keep this
place for them. The souls of the dead are no bigger
than a grain of wheat when they come, yet they too
like to have their back protected from the wind of
nothing, the wind of Descartes, and of all who grew
thin in maternal deprivation. Vigleik can come here,
with his lame knee, pinned in 1922 under a tree he
himself felled, rolling cigarettes with affectionate
fingers, patient and protective. And my brother can
sit here if he can find the time, he will bring his friend
if he comes; my grandmother will come here surely,
sometimes, with the ship she gave me. This balcony
is like her kitchen to the southwest, its cobstove full
of heating caves; and Olai with his favorite horse and
buggy, horsehide robe over his knees, ready to start
for town, with his mustache; the dead of the Civil
War, Thomas Nelson, fat as a berry, supported by
his daughters: and others I will not name I would
like to come. I will set out a drop of water and a grain
of rye for them. What the ants have worked out is
a place for our destiny, for we too labor, and no one
sees our labor. My father's labor who sees? It is in a
pasture somewhere not yet found by a walker. Mean-

while it is still open to the rains and snows. All labor still unfound is open to the rains and snows, who are themselves ants, who go into dark crevices and live.

III

The Grief of Men

The Buddhist ordered his boy to bring him, New
       Year's
morning, a message. He
woke; answered;
tore open the message
he himself had written, and signed, "Buddha."

"Busyness has caught you, you have slowed and
        stopped.
If you start toward me, I
will surely come
to meet you." He wept.
Exhausted by work and travel, I walk.

I hear the coot call his darkening call,
and the dog's doubt far back in his throat.
A porcupine walks
by the water at dusk;
no one sees him, under the low bushes.

Men have died on high slopes, as others watch.
They look around, and do not see
those they love most,
and call out
the sound the porcupine does not make.

And fresh waters wash past the tidal sands,
into the delta, wash past clear
bars and are gone.
Women can die
in childbirth, Bertha, inwardly near me, died,

my father's sister. "No more children, that's it,"
the doctor said. They wanted a child.
The doctor stands
by the bed, but Bertha
dies, her breath ends, her knees quiver and are still.

Her husband will not lie quiet.
He throws himself against the wall.
Men come to hold him down.
My father is there,
sits by the bed long night after night.

Kennedy's Inauguration

The Sister hands it to me—the seed
of the sweet-gum tree.
New to me, it is the size
of a cow's eyeball.
Dry as a pinecone, round
and brown. Its seeing
is all gone, finished,
exploded out
through the eye-holes.
I turn it in my palm,
it pricks the tender skin.

Dry spikes, beaklike
splinters—hen
beaks widening in fear.
Are the dogs
coming? Where an eye
should be, another
beak is opening, where
an ear should be,
a beak is opening—blindness
and deafness
make the cries more hoarse.

And what did I do today?
I drove on errands
twice so as not to pass
the funeral home;
I had three conversations,
all distant.
Well, if I know how to live,
why am I frightened?
I see Lorenzo's head
in my hand, cheek
broken by a cannonball,

one eye dangles out.
The Catholic
strangles the Papal candidate
with a thin cord.
King Leopold's plantation
men cut off
the boy's hands, punishing
the father for missing
work; the boy's hands
lie on the ground
at the father's feet.

In Nineteen Thirty-Eight
Brown Shirts
arrive, smash the contra-
ceptive clinics,
take women away
into breeding hotels.
I look down: Marilyn
Monroe is there.
The arm of the drugged mistress
hangs out a hole
over the side of the bed.

Out of her back comes the Marine's
cry for the medic.
His foot is lying a few
feet away,
his lips are open, the brain
is missing—only
the throat and cry are there.
And the President
in the cold—the old white-
haired poet nearby—
lays one hand on the Bible.

Written at Mule Hollow, Utah

for Robert and Ollie

After three days of talk, I long for silence and come
      here.
It's called Mule Hollow. I love this granite steep
      shooting
upward. The base seems to remain
in grief—all the children killed when you return to
      the cave.

Haven't you ever longed for all these cheerful noises
to end? These hellos and good-byes? We fall asleep
      speaking.
Perhaps talking we sleep;
our ability to wake stays hidden in rocks that we
      never visit.

This tree I stand beside—a stone wall behind it,
sedimentary, moving in waves—it is neither tree nor
      pine;
it has half-leaves, half-needles,
and a scaly bark, like someone constantly waking up
      in the night.

All the failures of the stone are perfectly clear—
    spoken—
how it gave way to pressures, bent between humps,
as when a man lets his hands
climb over his head, and says, "It's true, it's true,
    why say it isn't?"

How many failures we hide, talking. When I am too
    public,
I am a wind-chime, ringing, to cheer up the black
Angel Moroni, and feed him
as he comes dancing, prancing, leaving turkey tracks
    in the mist.

Talking, we do not say what we are! Sensing what
    others want,
used to hiding from our parents, talking,
not saying what we want,
we sustain the brilliant glass skeleton on which we
    hang.

What the Fox Agreed to Do

1

Herbs, turtle-faced porcupine babies,
fur, pawmarks on shore,
the hair in the mouse's ear.

2

This descent is the wheeling of the inexhaustible
bear, whose furry tail
dips again and again into the ocean.

3

And we are rheumatic pilgrims, stalking
in the night air,
driving flocks of angel cattle before them.

4

Long seeds drop into November loam.
The mother throws off her clothes, descending—
the Virgin is lost among the other stars.

5

And the shells, the mollusc shells, grow large.
Smoke twists up through water,
the moon rockets up from the sea floor.

6

The fox agrees to leap into the ocean.
The human being feels a splash around him.
Hebrews straddle the slippery dolphins.

Words Rising

for Richard Eberhart

I open my journal, write a few
sounds with green ink, and suddenly
fierceness enters me, stars
begin to revolve, and pick up
alligator dust from under the ocean.
The music comes, I feel the bushy
tail of the Great Bear
reach down and brush the sea floor.

All those lives we lived in the sunlit
shelves of the Dordogne, the thousand
tunes we sang to the skeletons
of Papua, the many times
we died - wounded - under the cloak
of an animal's sniffing, all of these
return, and the grassy nights
we ran in the moonlight for hours.

Watery syllables come welling up.
Anger that barked and howled in the cave,
the luminous head of barley
the priest holds up, growls
from under fur, none of that is lost!
The old earth fragrance remains
in the word "and." We experience
"the" in its lonely suffering.

We are bees then; language is the honey.
Now the honey lies stored in caves
beneath us, and the sound of words
carries what we do not.
When a man or woman feeds a few words
with private grief, the shames we knew
before we could invent
the wheel, then words grow. We slip out

into farmyards, where rabbits lie
stretched out on the ground for buyers.
Wicker baskets and hanged men
come to us as stanzas and vowels.
We see a million hands with dusty
palms turned up inside each verb,
lifted. There are eternal vows
held inside the word "Jericho."

Blessing them on the man who labors
in his tiny room, writing stanzas on the lamb;
blessings on the woman, who picks the brown
seeds of solitude in afternoon light
out of the black seeds of loneliness.
And blessings on the dictionary maker, huddled
          among
his bearded words, and on the setter of songs
who sleeps at night inside his violin case.

A Sacrifice in the Orchard

The man with the Roman nose sits high
on the roof ridge, longs for it
to be Saturday. And moles
begin crossing the lawn,
thousands of moles,
the grief-stricken parents
come behind in closed cars.
Come with me, we will
sink on this blue raft
down through acres
of continental water. Shaggy
goats bound from the earth.
Over them, men
hang from the branches.
They are all apples. The side
of the apple gleams,
and in that gleam
all the water on the planet
plunges down at once. . . .

A Meditation on Philosophy

There is a restless gloom in my mind.
I walk grieving. Leaves are down.
I come at dusk
where, sheltered by poplars, a low pond lies.
The sun abandons the sky, speaking through colc
        leaves.

A deer comes down the slope toward me,
sees me, turns away, back up the hill
into the lone trees.
It is a doe out in the cold and air alone,
the woman turned away from the philosopher's
        house.

Someone wanted that. After Heraclitus dies,
the males sink down to a-pathy,
to not-suffering.
When you shout at them, they don't reply.
They turn their face toward the crib wall, and die

A Tang painter made *The Six Philosophers.*
Five Chinamen talk in the open-walled house,
exchanging poems.
Only one is outdoors, looking over
the cliff, being approached from below by rolling
    mists.

It must be that five of me are indoors!
Yesterday, when I cleaned my study,
I laid your paints,
watercolor paper, sketches and sable brushes
not on the bookcase, where mine were, but on the
    floor.

But there are thunderstorms longing to come
into the world through the minds of women!
One bird of yours came,
it was a large friendly bird with big feet,
stubby wings, and arrows lightly stuck in the arms.

Last night I dreamt that my father
was an enormous turtle—the eyes open—
lying on the basement floor.
The weight of his shell kept him from moving.
His jaw hung down—it was large and fleshly.

My Father's Wedding
1924

Today, lonely for my father, I saw
a log, or branch,
long, bent, ragged, bark gone.
I felt lonely for my father when I saw it.
It was the log
that lay near my uncle's old milk wagon.

Some men live with an invisible limp,
stagger, or drag
a leg. Their sons are often angry.
Only recently I thought:
Doing what you want . . .
Is that like limping? Tracks of it show in sand.

Have you seen those giant bird-
men of Bhutan?
Men in bird masks, with pig noses, dancing,
teeth like a dog's, sometimes
dancing on one bad leg!
They do what they want, the dog's teeth say that!

But I grew up without dogs' teeth,
showed a whole body,
left only clear tracks in sand.
I learned to walk swiftly, easily,
no trace of a limp.
I even leaped a little. Guess where my defect is!

Then what? If a man, cautious
hides his limp,
Somebody has to limp it! Things
do it; the surroundings limp.
House walls get scars,
the car breaks down; matter, in drudgery, takes it up.

On my father's wedding day,
no one was there
to hold him. Noble loneliness
held him. Since he never asked for pity
his friends thought he
was whole. Walking alone, he could carry it.

He came in limping. It was a simple
wedding, three
or four people. The man in black,
lifting the book, called for order.
And the invisible bride
stepped forward, before his own bride.

He married the invisible bride, not his own.
In her left
breast she carried the three drops
that wound and kill. He already had
his barklike skin then,
made rough especially to repel the sympathy

he longed for, didn't need, and wouldn't accept.
They stopped. So
the words are read. The man in black
speaks the sentence. When the service
is over, I hold him
in my arms for the first time and the last.

After that he was alone
and I was alone.
No friends came; he invited none.
His two-story house he turned
into a forest,
where both he and I are the hunters.

Four Ways of Knowledge

So many things happen
when no one is watching.
Yesterday a friend and I
arrived on the island
to visit Iolani Luahine.
We couldn't find her.
Later that night, he
left the room, flew,
saw the temple ahead,
but grew tired, faltered,
turned back,
caught the balcony
railing, pulled himself in.
Inside the room
a woman with claw
feet and hands met him.
What to do . . . to stall her.
To fight or to flee—
He didn't know. He wanted
to fight *and* to flee.
His feet in tennis shoes
moved back and forth,

rubbing the carpet.
I awoke at four, hearing
the sound of shoe soles
scuffling the soft rug.
The other sleeper was still asleep
and in his bed. When
I spoke his name, the sound
stopped. At breakfast,
he said: "I dreamt. . . ."
Now I have gone alone
to write by the ocean,
and watch the fish
between rocks.
I feel my eyes
open below the water.
Some power I cannot see
moves these small fish.
The sunlit ocean approaches
and recedes, rolling in
on its black lava base.
Things happen
when no one is watching,
perhaps *because*
no one is watching.
Pirates bring their ship in
when night has come;
the dancer becomes beautiful
when men see her
no longer. Earth

is a thicket of thistles
waiting for the Wild Man.
Everything is in motion,
even what is still.
The planet turns, and the cows
wait for the grassblades
to come rushing to their mouths.
Someone tries to teach us.
In childhood, he calls us
each day to remember
one or two things only.
I remember I fell
one Sunday from my parents'
car, I saw it leaving
me on the road, going.
My parents do not recall it.
If we ignore that, he
waits till we are asleep,
opens the images, borrows
faces, turns men to turtles—
I dreamt that I sat
in a chair, and every other
second I disappeared.
But what if we lose the dream?
Then he starts to do it
on his own, books fall
open to a certain passage,
two strangers in one day
speak the same sentence.

The telephone rings after the funeral.
Insubstantial molecules turn
heavy, become tennis shoes.
If we still don't
take in the knowledge,
then he turns to accidents,
disease, suffering,
lost letters, torpid sleeps,
disasters, catatonia.
We walk, the glass
mountain opens, we fall in.
I usually ignore the other
three, and learn by falling.
This time we live it,
and only awaken years later.

Fifty Males Sitting Together

After a long walk in the woods clear cut for lumber,
lit up by a few young pines,
I turn home,
drawn to water. A coffinlike shadow
softens half the lake,
draws the shadow
down from westward hills.
It is a massive
masculine shadow,
fifty males sitting together
in hall or crowded room
lifting something indistinct
up into the resonating night.

Closer to me, out of shadow, the water lies lit,
some of it pinkish from western clouds.
Near shore, reeds
stand about in groups, unevenly,
as if they might finally
and at once ascend
to the sky all together!
A thin thread

of darkness lives
in each reed, so it is relaxed,
private. When the reed dies,
it dies alone, as an animal does.
Rooted, it waits only for itself.

The woman stays in the kitchen, and does not want
to waste fuel by lighting a lamp,
as she waits for the drunk
husband to come home.
Then leaving the kitchen
dark, she
serves him food in silence.
Nearly at my feet,
motionless water
lies calm, protected by reeds.
So the son who lives
protected by the mother lives protected
by reeds in the joy of the half-darkness.

He lives thousands of years ago. He does not
      know
what he should give, as herds slowly
pass the cave mouth,
what the world *wants* from him.
Blood rises from dark
neck-holes.

But how far he lives
from working men!
The blood asks:
Whose head has been cut off?
The dark comes down slowly, the way
snow falls . . . or herds pass the cave.
I look up at the other shore; it is night.

Crazy Carlson's Meadow

Crazy Carlson cleared this meadow alone.
Now three blue-
jays live in it.
Crazy Carlson cleared it back to the dark firs.
Volunteer poplars have stepped
out in front,
their leaves trembling.
They hold their leaves in the motionless October air,

color midway between pale green and yellow,
as if a yellow
scarf were floating
six inches down in the Pacific. The dark firs
make sober, octopus caves,
deathlike, the heavy-
lidded eyes
of the women in whose bark huts Gauguin lived.

A blue sky rises over the trees, pure blue,
too pure and blue.
There is no room
for the dark-lidded boys who longed to be Hercules.
There is no room even for Christ.
He broke off
his journey toward the Father,
and leaned back into the mother's fearful tree.

Then he sank through the bark. The energies the
        Jews
refused him
turned into nails,
and the wine of Cana turned back to vinegar.
Blessings on you, my king, broken
on the poplar tree.
Your shoulders quivered
like an aspen leaf before the storm of Empire.

You fell off then, and the horse galloped away
into the wind without
you, and disappeared
into the blue sky. Your horse never reached your
        father's house.
But the suffering is over now, all
consequences finished,
the lake closed
again, as before the leaf fell, all forgiven, the path
        ended.

Now each young man wanders in the sky alone,
ignoring the absent
moon, not knowing
where ground is, longing once more for the learning
of the fierce male who hung for nine days only
on the windy tree.
Beneath his feet
there is darkness; inside the folds of darkness words
    hidden.

Kneeling Down to Look into a Culvert

I kneel down to peer into a culvert.
The other end seems far away.
One cone of light floats in the shadowed water.
This is how our children will look when we are dead.

I kneel near floating shadowy water.
On my knees, I am half inside the tunnel—
blue sky widens the far end—
darkened by the shadowy insides of the steel.

Are they all born? I walk on farther;
out in the plowing I see a lake newly made.
I have seen this lake before . . . it is a lake
I return to each time my children are grown.

I have fathered so many children and returned
to that lake—grayish flat slate banks,
low arctic bushes. I am a water-serpent, throwing
        water drops
off my head. My gray loops trail behind me.

How long I stay there alone! For a thousand years
I am alone, with no duties, living as I live.
Then one morning a feathery head pokes from the
    water.
I fight—it's time—it's right—and am torn to pieces
    fighting.

About the Author

Robert Bly was born in Minnesota and took his college work at St. Olaf and Harvard. In 1958 he founded a poetry magazine, which has been called, successively, *The Fifties, The Sixties, The Seventies,* and *The Eighties.* Among his books of poetry are *Silence in the Snowy Fields, The Light Around the Body,* which won the National Book Award, *Sleepers Joining Hands, The Morning Glory, This Body Is Made of Camphor and Gopherwood,* and *This Tree Will Be Here for a Thousand Years.* Bly has also published important translations including *The Kabir Book: 44 of the Ecstatic Poems of Kabir, Neruda and Vallejo: Selected Poems* (with James Wright and John Knoepfle), and the recent major work, *Selected Poems of Rainer Maria Rilke.* He is at work now on a collection of love poems, a book of selected essays, and a book exploring the psychic implications for men of some classic fairy tales.